MICHAEL ANDRETTI AT INDIANAPOLIS

BY MICHAEL ANDRETTI

WITH ROBERT & DOUGLAS CARVER
PHOTOGRAPHS BY DOUGLAS CARVER

SIMON & SCHUSTER BOOKS FOR YOUNG READERS
PUBLISHED BY SIMON & SCHUSTER
NEW YORK · LONDON · TORONTO · SYDNEY · TOKYO · SINGAPORE

ACKNOWLEDGMENTS

The authors would like to thank Tom Smith, Tom Wurtz and Ed Nathman of Newman-Haas Racing, Don Henderson of Andretti Management, Amy Hollowbush of MA500, Inc., Roger Deppe and Ellen Kline of the Indianapolis Motor Speedway, Elaine Brandin and Gail Dailey of Nikon Professional Services, Richard Taylor of Toshiba America, Jim Rogers of Volkswriter, Paul Christensen of Paul Christensen Studios, Sylvia Frezzolini of Westerly, Rhode Island, and Pamela Pollack of Simon & Schuster.

All photographs by Douglas Carver except for pages 12, 34–35, 36, 37, 38, 39 (top), 43, 45, 51 by Robert Carver; page 20 by Paul Christensen; endpapers and pages 4, 6, and 13 by Indianapolis Motor Speedway Corporation; and page 7 by Barnet of The Stars and Stripes.

This publication not affiliated with or authorized by Indianapolis Motor Speedway Corporation. Indy,™ Indy 500®, The Greatest Spectacle In Racing®, Indianapolis 500®, and Gasoline Alley® are trademarks of Indianapolis Motor Speedway Corporation.

SIMON & SCHUSTER BOOKS FOR YOUNG READERS
Simon & Schuster Building, Rockefeller Center
1230 Avenue of the Americas, New York, New York 10020

Designed by Sylvia Frezzolini
Manufactured in the United States of America
10 9 8 7 6 5 4 3 2   (pbk) 10 9 8 7 6 5 4 3 2 1

Library of Congress Cataloging-in-Publication Data
Andretti, Michael. Michael Andretti at Indianapolis / by Michael Andretti with Robert and Douglas Carver: photographs, Douglas Carver. Summary: Race car driver Michael Andretti recounts his experience participating in the 1991 Indy 500, a race in which his famous father Mario, his cousin John, and his brother Jeff also competed. 1. Indianapolis Speedway Race— Juvenile literature. 2. Indianapolis Speedway Race—Pictorial works—Juvenile literature. 3. Andretti, Michael—Juvenile literature. 4. Andretti, Michael—Pictorial works— Juvenile literature. [1. Indianapolis Speedway Race. 2. Andretti, Michael.] I. Carver Robert, 1953– . II. Carver, Douglas, ill. III. Title. GV1033.5.I55A54 1992
796.7'2'06877252—dc20   91-38815 CIP

ISBN: 0-671-75296-0   ISBN: 0-671-79674-7 (pbk)

To my wife, Sandy, and our children,
Marco and Marissa — MA

To my parents and my brothers — DC

To my parents and my children — RC

Race car engines sound like a cross between a roaring tiger and a purring cat: powerful and smooth at the same time.

Driving race cars is my job. Ever since I was a child, racing has been the only thing that I've ever wanted to do. When I was growing up, Mom would take the three of us—my brother, Jeff; my sister, Barbie; and me—to the track to watch Dad race.

My dad is Mario Andretti, the only hero I've ever had. Dad has won some of the biggest auto races and championships in the world: the Daytona 500, the Sebring 12 Hours of Endurance, and the Formula One World Championship. He has been so successful in racing that the street where he lives has been renamed Victory Lane.

In 1969, when I was six years old, I watched Dad win the Indianapolis 500. I was so excited and proud of him. Ever since that day, Indy has been the race I've most wanted to win.

During summer vacations in Pennsylvania at our lake, I'd race my minibike along the dirt trails until I was covered with dust. By the age of nine I was racing go-carts. The trophy that I won at the Pocono track in 1972 was almost as big as I was. I felt so proud when Dad congratulated me.

During my seven years of go-carting, I won twice as many races as I lost. Those victories fueled my love of racing.

My cousin John, whose father was also a race driver, developed an early interest in racing, too. We spent a lot of time learning together and competing against each other. John's been a good friend ever since.

Part of racing is driving at the limits. Each season as I've faced better drivers and new challenges, I've learned how to create opportunities to win. Discipline is part of the winning formula. Nobody wins without taking well-thought-out risks, but there's no excuse for taking foolish chances.

In 1980 I moved up to the Formula Ford series. I learned enough in my first year to win the Northeast Division championship the next year. In 1982 I won the Super Vee championship, and then in 1983 the Formula Mondial championship. Later in '83, Dad and I drove a Porsche in the 24 Hours of Le Mans. We finished third and I felt great: At the age of twenty I had become good enough to be my dad's teammate.

However, when I started racing in the Indy Car World Series, I noticed that there was a big jump in the quality of the drivers. I drove a few races in 1983, but my first race at Indianapolis wasn't until '84.

There's no place like the Indianapolis Motor Speedway. When the team and I arrive in early May, there aren't many people around. Then, during Memorial Day weekend, Indy becomes the site of the largest single-day sporting event in the world. Over 450,000 race fans surround the $2^{1}/_{2}$-mile track. For them it's a three-day carnival of high-speed entertainment. For the teams it's the ultimate test at the end of months of hard work. You can feel the energy in the air.

The racetrack is an oval with four turns and four flat straightaways. The two long straightaways are called the front and back straights, while the two shorter straights are known as short chutes. The four turns, or corners, are numbered one through four. They are banked nine degrees so that the inside of the track is lower than the outside.

Alongside the front straight is the pit area, where the cars are refueled and the engines are adjusted between laps. The garage area is the place where the race cars are stored and the major mechanical work is done. It is located behind the pits in the 320-acre infield. The infield is so big that there is even a golf course in it.

This is the seventy-fifth year of racing at the Indianapolis Motor Speedway. The Indianapolis 500 is one of the oldest auto races still in existence. The prize money is the largest in the world—over one million dollars goes to the winner. It is also rich in nicknames: Indy, the Indy 500, the Greatest Spectacle in Racing. The track is also known as the Speedway and the Brickyard (because originally the track surface was paved with bricks instead of asphalt. In fact, if you look closely, you will see that the start-finish line is still made of bricks).

The race at Indy is actually one of a series of races that are held at different tracks during the season, which runs from spring to fall. After every race each driver is awarded points according to his finishing position. The driver with the most points at the end of the season wins the year's national championship title.

Some races are on road courses, which are tracks with left and right turns. Some are run on city streets that have been set up for racing, while others, like Indy, are on large ovals built just for racing. The race at Indy is five hundred miles, or two hundred laps, long. A typical lap speed averages over 215 miles an hour.

Teams are a very important part of racing. I enjoy being acknowledged by the fans, but there is no doubt that winning is a team effort. Dad and I have been driving together for three years for the Newman-Haas team, which is co-owned by Paul Newman and Carl Haas. It has been a dream come true for me. Having Jeff and John also competing in the series makes racing a family experience, and I enjoy that, too.

Although Dad and I are the only Newman-Haas drivers, we have five nearly identical race cars: two for racing, two for backup, and one for spare parts. Our cars are made by Lola and our engines are by Chevrolet. Dad drives car number 6. I drive car number 10—in racing language, the Kmart-Havoline Lola-Chevrolet for the Newman-Haas team.

Why is my car called by all these names? It is because racing cars is very expensive. By the end of this year's season, the Newman-Haas team will have spent millions of dollars to compete at the seventeen events. To pay for all of this, the team owners make deals with different companies. These companies, called sponsors, give the team money and/or equipment in exchange for having their company's name or product promoted during the races. That is why company names are painted on the sides of race cars. The two biggest sponsors of the Newman-Haas team are the Kmart retail chain and Texaco Refining & Marketing Company, the manufacturer of Havoline oil.

The cars are built and maintained by crews. The Newman-Haas team has two crews, one for Dad's car and one for mine. There are ten crew

members who work on my car, each one a specialist. Ed Nathman, the
team manager, sees to the needs, schedules, and supplies of both crews.
Colin Duff, the chief mechanic, supervises the overall preparation of our
cars. Brian Lisles, the engineer, is responsible for my car's mechanical
settings. Tom Wurtz, my crew chief, makes sure that all of Brian's
decisions are carried out accurately and swiftly.

There are a lot of rules and regulations in racing. Before my car is allowed onto the track for practice, it must pass a technical inspection. United States Auto Club officials check the weight, fuel capacity, and specifications of each race car to make sure that the car is safe and that no one has an unfair advantage.

In 1989 Dad and I were the first father-son team to race at Indianapolis. This year the Andrettis are setting another record. Four members of the

same family will be competing in the Indy 500: Dad; my cousin John; my brother Jeff; and myself.

John is driving car number 4, the Lola-Chevrolet owned by Jim Hall, a former driver known for his innovative racing car designs. John won this season's opening race—our competition from our go-cart days continues.

Jeff is driving car number 86, the Lola-Cosworth owned by Bruce Leven. This is Jeff's first year racing at Indy. Dad, John, and I are willing to offer advice, but Jeff usually works things out on his own.

The rules allow a maximum of thirty-three cars to compete on race day, but every year many more than that attempt to qualify. One at a time, each driver is given four laps on an empty track to drive as fast as he can. With only four laps, there is no time to make up for errors; and with an empty track, there is no room for excuses.

The speed of each lap is recorded by official track timers. They average the lap times in order to determine each driver's qualifying time. Qualifying times are posted on a tall electronic display in the pit area. The fastest car is awarded the best starting position, called the pole position, for race day. The second-fastest car is awarded the second-best starting position, and so on until the thirty-three-car field is full.

Finally, it is my turn to qualify. Now that the waiting is over, I focus only on my job. I am no longer aware of the pressure to perform.

Out on the track I have problems with the pop-off valve, which limits the pressure in the turbocharger. Whenever the valve opens, my engine's power drops and my speed is reduced. It is frustrating, but, fortunately, the problem isn't too bad. My car is handling very well, so I can keep up my speed. Our teamwork pays off. With a four-lap average of 220.943 miles per hour, I qualify fifth.

By the end of the first day of qualifying, Dad has placed third, John has taken seventh, and Jeff has captured eleventh to become the fastest rookie qualifier of the year.

I speak with my father, his crew chief, and his engineer about the handling of his car.

Although Dad and I have separate crews, our team shares information freely. Frequently, Dad, his engineer, Tony Cicale, and team members from both crews discuss the combination of adjustments, known as the setup, that can affect the car's performance.

Combining this information with data gathered by the on-board computer in my car, my engineer, Brian, decides what modifications should be made to improve my car's speed and handling.

Once the crew makes the necessary changes to my car, we test it. Then there are more discussions, more adjustments, and more tests. With hundreds of parts that need constant maintenance and adjustment, my race car is more like an airplane than a street car.

At Indy my car has a twenty-three-inch wing in front of each front tire and a forty-two-inch wing at the back of the car behind the rear tires. They control aerodynamics, the way the car passes through the air. The wings work just like airplane wings except they are adjusted to keep my car firmly on the ground and to give me more traction. My crew can change the size and angle of the wings. They can even change the shape of the wings by adding or removing aluminum strips, called trim tabs or wickers.

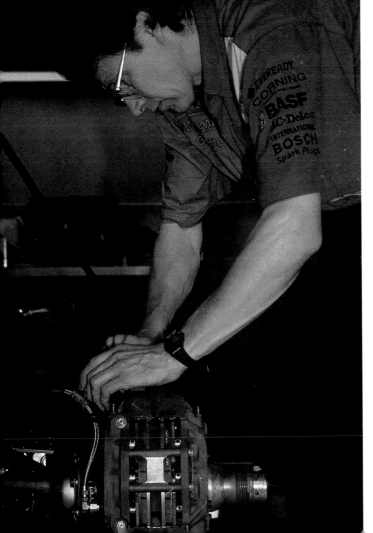

The framework of my car is called the chassis, or tub. The angle of my car's chassis in relation to the track surface is called the angle of attack. It must be carefully adjusted. Here at Indy, my car is a little lower on the left side, making the bottom of my car level with the tilt of the track corners. Both Dad and I have our chassis as close to the ground as the rules permit, so that we can go as fast as possible on the straightaways.

Even simple items, such as tires, require a full-time technician. Kenny "Retread" Szymanski is the crew member who takes care of the tires for all five Newman-Haas cars. During practice, qualifying, and the race, Dad and I will probably each use over thirty-five sets of Goodyear radial race tires; that's almost three hundred tires in one month.

Pointing tires straight ahead never yields the best performance, so my crew adjusts the direction of all four tires at each track. Usually, the wheels are mounted so that the tires point slightly inward, called toe-in. Tires that point outward are toe-out. Here at Indy, all four wheels on my car actually point in different directions in order to improve the car's handling.

Kenny and crew member Don "Tex" Textor also measure the size of each tire so that the difference, or stagger, between the height of the left and right rear tires can be adjusted. Since the track at Indy has four left turns and no right turns, having a taller right rear tire and a shorter left rear tire makes it easier for me to turn left.

During the race, I'm scheduled to make a pit stop every twenty-seven or twenty-eight laps. Because the time spent refueling the car and changing the tires during these stops can mean the difference between winning and finishing second, we always practice our pit stops before the race.

A low wall divides the pit area: The tools, spare tires, and refueling tanks are on one side; the race cars are on the other. For safety reasons, only six crew members are allowed on the car side of the wall during the race.

Parked in the pits with the air jacks extended, my car floats inches above the asphalt

My pit crew and I practice changing tires

In order to save time during a pit stop, racing cars have built-in air jacks that lift them off the ground. As soon as I stop, a pressurized hose is connected to the top of my car. Instantly, my chassis is in the air, and my pit crew—Tom Wurtz, Tim Coffeen, Ray Sorenson, and Don Textor— each change one of my tires.

At the same time, Trevor Weston and Kenny Siwieck refuel my car through an opening in the side of the car, called a dry-break. The dry-break provides for greater refueling speed and safety: Methanol fuel enters through one hose, while air and spillage exit through a second hose.

On Saturday afternoon, the day before the race, our team holds a ceremony in our garage. Although Jeff is driving for another team, he joins us. For this moment he is an Andretti first and a competitor second. We set up an informal altar and Father Phil leads us in a prayer.

This will be my eighth Indy 500, and I know I'm ready to compete: I'm mentally prepared, my car is running well, and I have a very professional crew behind me. It's a good feeling.

As the morning of the race arrives, rain falls on the Speedway Motel roof overhead. I'm wide awake and dressed long before my eight thirty alarm sounds.

At eight forty-five, after a bowl of cereal, I call my team's garage to find out how the rain is affecting the day's schedule. Carl Dean, my dad's crew chief, answers the phone. "Morning, Mike. Everything's running about an hour behind schedule. The Speedway crews are drying the track with the jet engine blow driers right now."

The overcast sky makes me uneasy, because drivers do not race in the rain at Indy as they do at some other tracks. I want to race. I tell myself that the skies will clear. All I can think of is the race.

My wife, Sandra, dresses our four-year-old son, Marco, and our six-month-old daughter, Marissa, in junior driver's suits, which are replicas of mine. I try to relax by spending some time with my family at the motel.

Suddenly, it's time to go. After a quick good-bye hug, Sandra and I head for the track on my motor scooter, leaving Marco and Marissa behind with their grandmother.

On the way to the garage, I can feel the heaviness of the air. I smile. This is a good sign. Race car engines work well in humid air; the moisture helps produce more power.

As I weave my scooter through the huge crowd, Sandra points out some patches of blue sky. We are going to race today!

At about ten thirty we arrive at the garage area. It is still called Gasoline Alley even though Indy cars have used methanol fuel for years. Crowds of spectators have gathered in front of every garage to watch the crews make their final preparations. As I enter the Newman-Haas garage, I sign autographs for a few fans. They're very enthusiastic and full of good wishes.

Inside the garage, my crew and I review our race strategy one last time. At around eleven o'clock, the crew prepares to move my car and the pit equipment out of our garage. First, though, my car is towed to the garage area pumps, where it is filled with methanol fuel.

I remain behind in our garage and put on my fire-resistant long underwear and driver's suit. The heavy clothes make me feel even hotter in this humid weather, so I am a bit uncomfortable. I'll sweat about seven pounds of water weight during today's race, but this is a small price to pay for the protection that the suit provides. By regulation, all crew members wear fire suits on race day.

In honor of this unusual occasion when all four Andretti drivers are competing in the same race, Dad, Jeff, John, and I walk out to the pit area together. On the way we see A.J. Foyt. A.J. is a legend in racing; he's won Indy four times. As a kid, I used to watch him compete against Dad. I never thought that someday I would be racing against them both.

"I trust you old boys had your fun qualifying last week," I say, poking fun at A.J. and Dad, who are two of the oldest drivers in today's race.

"You think you kids can show us a thing or two today?" A.J teases, knowing that both Dad and he have qualified on the front row, ahead of us younger Andrettis.

"We'll let you know in the next few hours," I answer.

Surrounded by fans and media, A.J. Foyt walks to his race car

In the pits, Kenny Siwieck holds my helmet while my personal manager, Don Henderson, helps me put on some throw-away shields. During the race, I peel off these shields to remove the bugs and oil from my visor.

A lot is happening. A parade of celebrities circles the track. Press photographers are everywhere, but I hardly notice them.

At eleven forty-five the track is cleared and each team pushes its race car from the pit area to its starting position on the front straightaway. The cars are lined up three abreast in eleven rows to form the thirty-three car starting grid. Having qualified fifth, my car is in the center of the second row. With a faster qualifying speed of 221.818 MPH, Dad is in the first row, alongside Rick Mears in car number 3 and A.J. Foyt in car number 14. With 219.059, John is a row behind me; and Jeff, with 217.632, is a row behind John. There is one Andretti driver in each of the four front rows.

Once the cars are in place, Sandra and I walk out to the starting grid. Before she helps me put on my helmet, I put on my fireproof face mask. It makes me look as if I am a creature from a science-fiction movie, because only my eyes are visible.

At twelve o'clock the announcer calls for all drivers to report to their cars. I squeeze into my cockpit, and Tom buckles my seat belt. It has two shoulder straps, two waist straps, and a double strap between my legs. As soon as I'm comfortable, I check my gas, brake, and clutch pedals to make sure there aren't any last-minute problems.

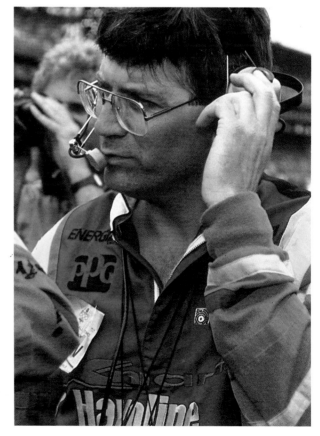

During the race, I can talk to my team manager, Ed Nathman, via the car radio. The microphone is built into the front of my helmet; the speaker is built into my right earplug.

Built into my left earplug is a hollow tube that connects to the engine's pop-off valve. By listening to the sound coming from the pop-off valve, I know whether I need to adjust the pressure of the air going into the engine. It's a simple but very helpful idea that Dad introduced to racing in 1981.

To the right of me in car number 2 is Al Unser, Jr. Al is from a racing family, too.

To my left is Bobby Rahal in car number 18. So far, Bobby has finished second in every race this season. I notice Roger Penske, team owner of Rick Mears's and Emerson "Emmo" Fittipaldi's cars, giving Bobby a thumbs-up sign as he passes.

Driver Bobby Rahal and team owner Roger Penske before the start of the race

Finally, Mrs. Mary Hulman, whose family owns the Indianapolis Motor Speedway, signals the beginning of the race with the phrase Indy has made famous: "Gentlemen, start your-r-r engines."

Instantly responding, nearly half a million spectators and thirty-three engines roar to life. With five times the power of an ordinary street car, the vibration of my 720-horsepower engine goes through my entire body.

I quickly check the gauges on my electronic dashboard: lap time, fuel remaining, fuel pressure, oil pressure, engine speed, water temperature, oil temperature, and boost, which indicates the pressure of the air entering the engine. Everything is okay.

Before the high-speed start of the race, a modified street car, called the pace car, leads the race cars, or field, around the track for three 110-MPH warm-up laps. During the pace laps, I carefully weave my car from side to side to heat up my tires in order to increase their traction.

As we enter Turn 4 of the last pace lap, I check the location of the cars around me. We're all looking for an opportunity to shoot ahead at the start, but none of us knows what his competitors will do.

Exiting Turn 4, the front row quickly picks up speed. I press down on the gas pedal, and the rest of the field accelerates behind me. I can see the green flag waving. Instantly, I shift my focus from waiting to winning.

The pace car enters the pit lane as the final pace lap begins

The seventy-fifth Indianapolis 500 has started, and we're *racing!*

The first corner of the first lap is the most dangerous. We are all bunched unusually close together, and we all want to be in the lead. Although the track widens to sixty feet in the corners, three cars abreast make the track feel as if it is narrowing like a funnel. I think to myself, "Jeff must be wide awake now." Not only is it his first race at Indy but he's used to starting races with two cars per row, not three.

Suddenly, disaster strikes. Gary Bettenhausen loses control and his car drifts sideways. Directly behind him, Buddy Lazier, the youngest driver in the field at age twenty-one, jams on his brakes, struggling to avoid Gary's spinning car. Smoke from burning rubber rises from their screeching tires as Buddy runs out of room and crushes the nose of his car into the outside wall. I'm safe because the two cars are behind me.

Immediately, yellow caution flags and lights are displayed around the track, signaling an unsafe condition. Racing is temporarily suspended and passing is prohibited. Before the completion of the first lap, Buddy is already out of the race and Gary has to pit for repairs.

The pace car returns to the track and we bunch up behind it, running slower laps of only 100 MPH. I do my best to avoid running over pieces of the damaged cars while the safety crews remove the dangerous accident debris.

Since the accident happened on the first lap, it is too early for any of us to pit for fuel or tires. My car is handling well—no need to stop for adjustments. I glance at the numbers on my dashboard; everything's fine. I call into the pits on my radio: "Ed, the car feels good and I'm okay."

Relieved, Ed replies, "Good, Michael, word is that no one was hurt too badly. I'll try to let you know when we'll be racing under the green flag again."

During the yellow flag condition, I feel like a jockey waiting for the starting gate to open. Finally, Ed comes back on the radio and says, "Get ready, Mike. I think the track is clear." As I start down the front straight, I see the green flag waving, returning us to racing speed.

Rick Mears is leading the race, but I can tell that his car is not handling well. I make a good restart, but Dad does even better: On the front straight of Lap 12, he passes Rick and takes the lead.

Rick continues to struggle with his car. Within a few laps I overtake him and move into second place. Running in second place with Dad in first feels very good. Only one thing could be better: if our positions were reversed and I was running first.

My father is in the lead as we head down the front straightaway

My father and I at the front of the field entering Turn One

Both John and Jeff are also within the top-ten positions. The Andrettis are really giving them a run for their money today, I tell myself.

I continue behind Dad for the next couple of laps as we pull away from the rest of the field. There's a lot more driving to be done before the race is over, but for now the rest of the field is no longer nipping at our exhaust pipes.

On Lap 24, Kevin Cogan, driving car number 9, and Roberto Guerrero, driving car number 40, brush against each other in Turn 1. Seconds later they both crash hard into the wall. Broken car parts shoot into the air. Seeing the accident, A.J. drives on the edge of the track in search of safety, but debris flying off one of the damaged cars crushes his left suspension and he's out of the race.

Kevin's and Roberto's cars spin across the track, scattering debris all along the short chute before they settle in the infield. Under the yellow caution flag, I slowly thread my way through the wreckage, taking great care to avoid hitting scraps that could easily puncture my tires or damage one of my radiators.

On the next lap, I see Roberto standing beside his car; he's okay. One lap later and Kevin is still not out of his car. Race cars are built with safety in mind, but since this has been such a high-speed accident, Kevin's battered car is surrounded by a safety crew and medical team. I hope that he's all right. (I later learn that Kevin was injured; but, fortunately, he received prompt medical care.)

Cars bunch up as safety workers clear accident debris from the track

Another nine laps pass before the track is clear. Finally, racing resumes on Lap 33. I see an opportunity. Immediately, I aim my car low on the inside of Turn 1. My strategy works. As Dad appears in my rearview mirror, the track ahead of me becomes wide open. I'm in the lead!

It's always a great feeling to be out in front. Dad may be my hero, but on the track we're in full competition. Until now I've been fighting the turbulent air created by the cars ahead of me. Now the air is undisturbed, so I enjoy a much smoother ride. Because there is no one left to pass, I concentrate on competing with myself. I feel a surge of energy. For the moment, life is perfect.

Competitors Arie Luyendyk (above) and Tony Bettenhausen (below)

Going into Turn 4, I remember the first time I ever led the field at Indy. It was the first lap of the 1986 race. As I left Turn 4, I hit an invisible wall of air turbulence left behind by the thirty-three cars at the start of the race. It was like driving into a hurricane. Hundreds of pounds of wind hit my car from different directions. I was caught completely by surprise and had to fight hard to control my car as I was thrown around inside my cockpit. It's an experience I'll never forget.

It's lap 78. I'm in sixth gear with my engine running at 11,700 RPM. Just as I begin to back off my accelerator in preparation for Turn 1, I notice teammate "Dashboard Dan" Toborg standing at the pit wall, holding up my signal board. It's time for me to make a pit stop. As I exit Turn 4 of the next lap, I bring my car low to the inside of the track and head for the pits. I was involved in a bad accident in the pits earlier this season, so I'm especially careful to avoid the other cars entering and exiting the pits.

During a pit stop I go from over 215 MPH to a full stop in a matter of seconds. Yet, as my car comes to a halt, my thoughts speed up; my mind is still racing.

My crew must perform with precision and speed, so we rarely speak. I concentrate on keeping my engine running; it is easy to stall a hot engine when the car isn't moving. Tom, Ray, Tim, and Tex change all my tires; Kenny and Trevor put in 37½ gallons of fuel. From the other side of the wall, "Delco Dick" Elmore passes me a refreshing drink of NutriQuest.

As soon as Tom gives me the go-ahead, I shift into first gear, rev up my engine, and, the instant the car is back on the ground, race off in a cloud of tire smoke—all in sixteen seconds. In another two seconds I'm going over 60 MPH and entering the track.

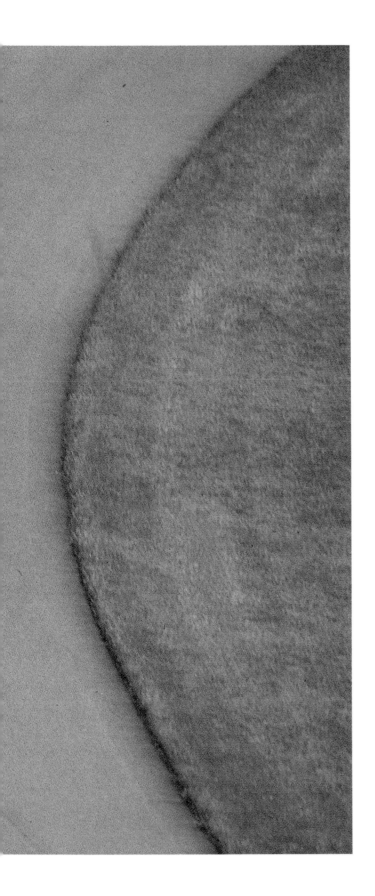

My pit stop is fast enough to allow me to regain the lead on the next lap when Al, Jr. pits. But the smooth air is gone, because I'm so far ahead that I'm starting to pass the slower cars that are still on the previous lap.

With average speeds between 216 and 221 MPH—which is like traveling the length of a football field in one second—I'm constantly jostled around inside my cockpit. Hundreds of pounds of pressure push me against the side of my cockpit in every corner. The crowd appears as a streaked blur of colors, making it hard for me to separate the red, yellow, and green traffic warning lights from the background. I blink my eyes and peel off one of my throw-away shields, and my vision improves.

The race is going very well for me. A full lap around the track takes about forty-one seconds. I have an eighteen-second lead, nearly half a lap. I look at my fuel gauge and read the numbers over the radio to Ed, so that he can check how many miles I'm getting per gallon.

I am now halfway into the race. I prepare to pass Rick Mears. If I can pass him, I'll be a full lap ahead of every car in the field. They'll have to pass me twice in order to win!

As I enter Turn 1, my car starts to drift sideways. Suddenly, the rear end is no longer stable; it slides toward the outside wall. I can tell that my left rear tire is losing traction. Caught in a battle to control my car, I'm forced to reduce my speed. Immediately, Rick begins to pull away from me. The turns seem a lot longer now than they were just a lap ago.

Although I have been in very little traffic for most of the race, I'm now in heavy traffic. Powerful gusts of air swirl off of the cars ahead of me. Suddenly, I have two problems: the loss of traction in my rear tire and the turbulent air ahead of me.

I call in over the radio: "Ed, my car's gone loose and it's getting worse. I'll need some adjustments when I stop." I don't want to waste valuable seconds for an unscheduled pit stop, so I add, "I'll stay out as long as I can."

"I read you, Mike. Ready when you are," Ed replies.

After about eight more laps, I'm losing more time by staying out on the track than I would be by coming in, so I enter the pits. In seconds, I'm parked. Kenny clicks the pressurized air hose into position, and my car pops up into the air. Four different power wrenches whirl into action. As soon as the wheel nuts are off, my worn tires are whisked away. Fresh tires take their place before the wheel nuts spin back on securely. My fuel tank is refilled and my front wings are adjusted. One by one, the fuel, vent, and pressure hoses are disconnected. My air jacks retract, dropping me back onto the pavement. I return to the race in third position.

However, before I even reach the track, Ed comes on the radio. "Mike, bad news. Your rear tire was cut. That's why the car was handling so poorly."

I'm stunned. Despite my best efforts, I must have run over a tiny piece of debris. We shouldn't have changed my front wing position. The setting was correct. But I'm even more upset at having been forced to make an unscheduled pit stop. If I had not lost those few precious seconds, I would have been able to pass Rick and get a full lap ahead of him.

I refuse to be distracted and settle in. It will be twenty-seven more laps before I can return my wing setting to its proper position.

John is in fifth place despite some minor car problems. I give him a quick wave as I pass him on the front straight.

Jeff is directly behind John, but on the 150th lap, his engine blows up, forcing him out of the race. He's unharmed but very disappointed. If he had been able to hold his position, he would have finished sixth.

I lead my cousin John down the front straightaway

My brother Jeff racing

I recapture the lead and hold it for eleven laps before making my next scheduled pit stop. The front wing setting is returned to its earlier position and the stagger, or height, of my right rear tire is increased to improve my car's handling in the turns. Eighteen seconds later I return to the race in third place behind Rick Mears and the current leader, Emerson "Emmo" Fittipaldi.

On Lap 169 Emmo enters the pits to refuel. He gets tires and fuel, but he has a mechanical problem that cannot be repaired quickly. He makes his best effort to leave the pits, but his car breaks down before reaching the track. In less than a minute Emmo has gone from leading the race to watching it from the pits.

Rick takes the lead and I move up into second. When Rick goes in for his pit stop, I return to first and concentrate on trying to build a strong

lead. By the 179th lap, I'm fourteen seconds ahead, but I know that I must make one more stop for fuel before the end of the race.

On the 185th lap, smoke streams from the engine of Danny Sullivan's car. He's out of the competition. But this is good for me: It allows me to make my final fuel stop under a yellow caution flag, which slows the field and minimizes the time I lose to my competitors.

Rick does regain the lead, but I return to the track and close up behind him. Fifteen laps remain when the safety lights change from yellow to green to restart the race. There's very little time left. Using the extra traction provided by my new tires, I make a bold move and drive high on the track, trying to overtake Rick in Turn 1.

Yes! I'm in the lead. I push my car to its limit, but Rick remains close behind me. The image of his car fills my rearview mirror.

On the next lap, Rick is directly behind me as we head down the front straight. As we enter Turn 1, Rick drives high on the track and probably hopes his tires have enough traction to get him through the corner. He's making the same move I made the lap before. It works for him, too. With twelve laps remaining, I'm back in second place.

Then, without warning, Dad's engine fails. Unable to make it into the pits, he drives his car off the track. The yellow caution signal returns.

I had been hoping that Rick would have to stop for more fuel, but this is the second caution within the last thirty laps. Each caution slows the race and reduces fuel consumption, so Rick will be able to finish the race without another pit stop.

A few laps later, we have a green flag. Rick and I are the only cars on the lead lap. I'm circling the track faster than I have all day, but I'm still not going fast enough. Rick is too fast for me to catch. As I exit Turn 4 of the two hundredth lap and head for the finish line, I watch Rick cross it 3.149 seconds ahead of me. The checkered victory flag waves back and forth, announcing Rick's fourth Indy 500 win.

I drive the customary cool-down lap filled with frustration and disappointment. I worked so hard to win, yet I finished second with Rick only a thousand feet ahead of me.

During the race, I led nearly three times as many laps as any other driver. My crew worked faster in the pits than any other team. It had been a perfect day—except for my cut tire. The tire kept me from lapping Rick and forced me to make an additional pit stop. Yet I know that if's, and's, and but's don't win races. We were beaten by one of the best team-driver combinations in the business.

The winner's circle at Indy is only big enough for one. There is no celebration for me or Arie Luyendyk, who finished third.

There is an award banquet the following evening for the team owners and drivers. We swap jokes and stories before the formal ceremony begins. Jeff contributes to the Andretti legend, winning honors as rookie of the year, just as Dad had in 1965 and I had in 1984.

As soon as the ceremony is completed, the Andretti family leaves for the airport. It's been a long month of hard work. Besides, we have a race in Milwaukee next weekend.

Michael competing at his hometown track, the Pennsylvania International Raceway, in Nazareth, PA.

At the Champion Spark Plug 300, the last race of the 1991 season, Michael Andretti qualified fastest, led 83 out of 84 laps to win his eighth season victory, and established a record for total laps led (881 out of 2,023). Although he has been runner-up three times, this was Michael's first Indy Car championship.

He continued to dominate the Indy Car World Series throughout 1992, winning more races and starting pole positions, and leading more than half of the total laps raced during the '92 season.

The 1992 Indy 500 was an accident-filled race due to unusually cold temperatures. Michael dominated the race until a broken pump belt forced him out only twelve laps from the finish.

Mechanical problems kept him from completing four other races. The 1992 championship remained undecided until the last race of the season. There, Michael won the pole and led the race from start to finish, but still ended the season four points behind Bobby Rahal, the 1991 Indy Car runner-up.

In 1993 Michael will begin a new challenge and follow in his father's footsteps: driving in the Formula One Grand Prix racing circuit, an international competition of Indy-type racing cars.